Whitney Waits Tables

(Sort Of!)

Marcy Schaaf

This story is more than just words on a page—it's a cherished memory from my heart. It all happened in Flint, Michigan, where my daughter Whitney spent many afternoons with her paternal grandmother, lovingly called "Grandma Ha."

Grandma Ha wasn't just a grandmother; she was a force of nature—kind, resourceful, and always full of life. She owned a small restaurant in town, a place that smelled like fresh bread and warm soup, where laughter filled the air and friends were always welcome.

One particular day stands out vividly in my mind. I was working late, and Whitney was spending the day with her Grandma Ha, as she often did. But this day was different—the waitress called in sick, leaving Grandma Ha shorthanded. Rather than fret, Grandma Ha turned to her little helper, Whitney, and gave her a notepad, a pen, and a warm smile.

What happened next was pure magic. Whitney, with her endless curiosity and determination, stepped up in a way that melted my heart. She not only helped her grandma take orders but brought joy to everyone in the café that day.

When I came to pick Whitney up, Grandma Ha handed me $50 in tips that Whitney had earned. It wasn't the money that struck me—it was the pride on Whitney's face, the gratitude in Grandma Ha's voice, and the warmth of knowing they had shared something so special.

This story is about more than helping out at a restaurant. It's about the bond between a grandmother and her granddaughter, the lessons we learn from our family, and the power of a grateful and giving heart.

I hope as you read this, you'll feel the same love and joy we did that day in Flint, Michigan. May it remind us all to cherish the moments with our loved ones and to always be ready to lend a helping hand with a happy heart.

Whitney loved her Grandma Ha,
Who owned a café near and far.

While Mom was busy working away,
Whitney stayed with Ha all day.

One sunny day, oh what a sight,
Grandma Ha faced a café fright!
Cafe

The waitress called,
"I'm sick, I'm done!"
Grandma said,
"Whitney, let's have some fun!"

She handed a pad and a pen to Whitney. "Take the orders, dear, quick and nifty!"

Whitney nodded and gave a smile.
"I'll help out; it'll be worthwhile!"

She walked to a table and said with cheer,
"What would you like to eat, my dear?"

Then she climbed up high in
the booth so snug,
"How do you spell that? A
sandwich or mug?"

Grandma Ha in the kitchen heard
it all,
She whipped up dishes, big and
small.

Whitney ran back with the note in hand,
"Good job!" said Ha, "You're so grand!"

Grandma Ha gave her
colors bright,
"Draw for the guests, give
them delight!"

Whitney sketched a dog, a sun, a tree,
The guests clapped and tipped with glee!

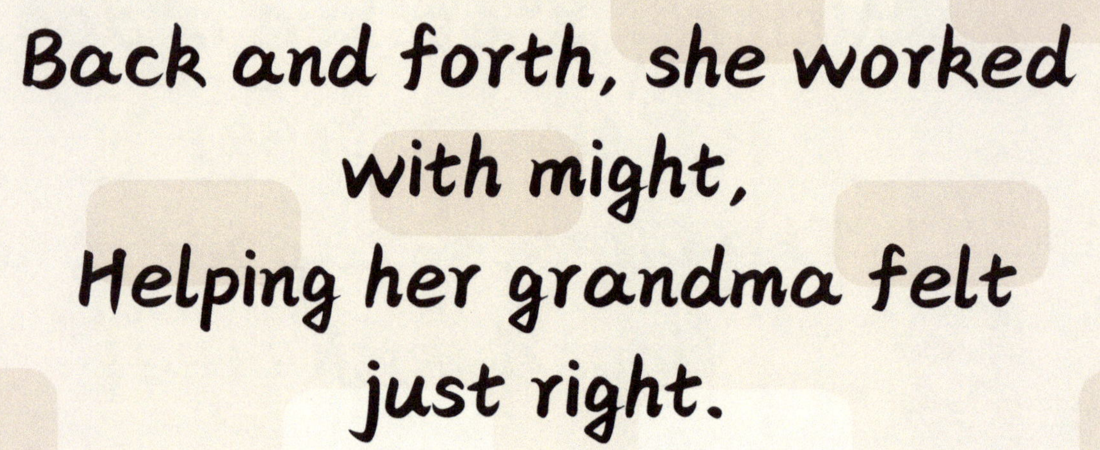

Back and forth, she worked
with might,
Helping her grandma felt
just right.

When Mom came back to pick Whitney up, Grandma Ha said, "Here's her tip cup!"

Cafe

Fifty dollars! Mom said,
"Oh my!
You're such a helper; I
could cry!"

Whitney grinned and gave a hug,
She felt so proud, all warm and snug.

Grandma Ha said,
"Whitney, you see,
Helping with love brings joy
and glee."

Whitney said,
"Thank you, Ha, you're the best!
Spending time with you beats all
the rest!"

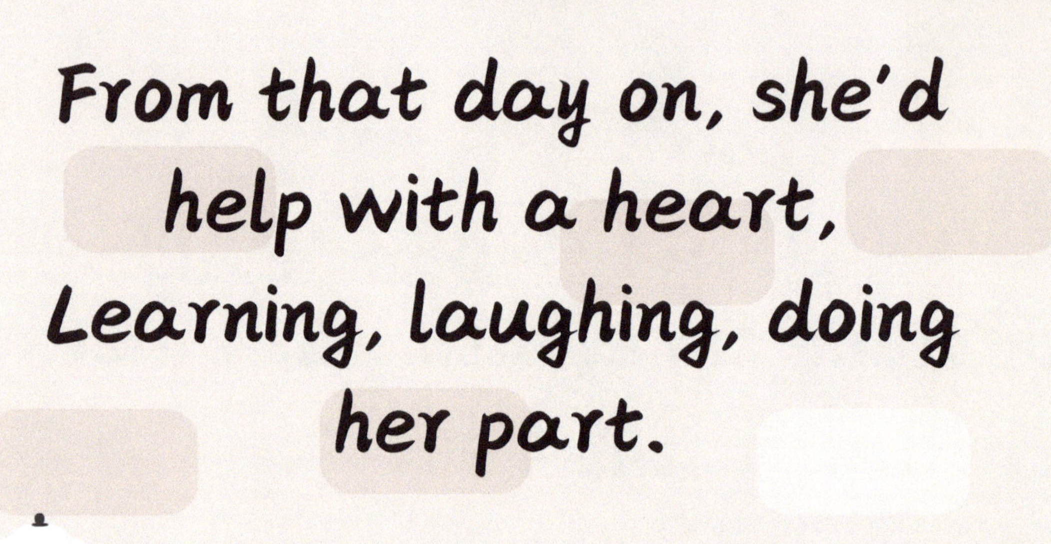

From that day on, she'd
help with a heart,
Learning, laughing, doing
her part.

The lesson Whitney learned
that day:
Kindness and effort light
the way.

So if your grandma needs a
hand,
Say, "I'm here! Let's make
a plan!"

Whitney worked hard with joy and cheer,
Making memories year by year.

Grandma Ha and her little
helper too,
Ran the café like a dream
come true!

Helping out isn't just for play,
It brings big smiles to every day.

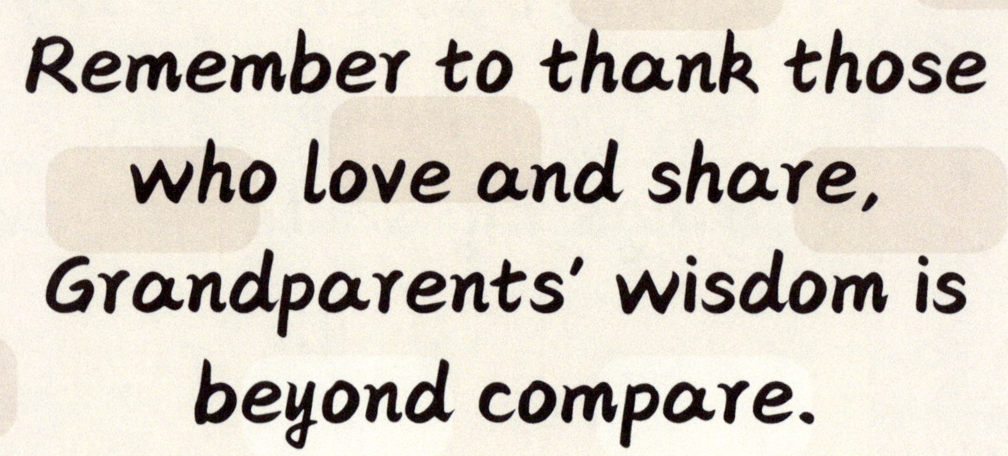

Remember to thank those
who love and share,
Grandparents' wisdom is
beyond compare.

Cafe

Whitney knew, as she grew tall,
Helping Grandma was the best gift of all!

So when you're with your grandma dear,
Lend a hand, bring joy and cheer.

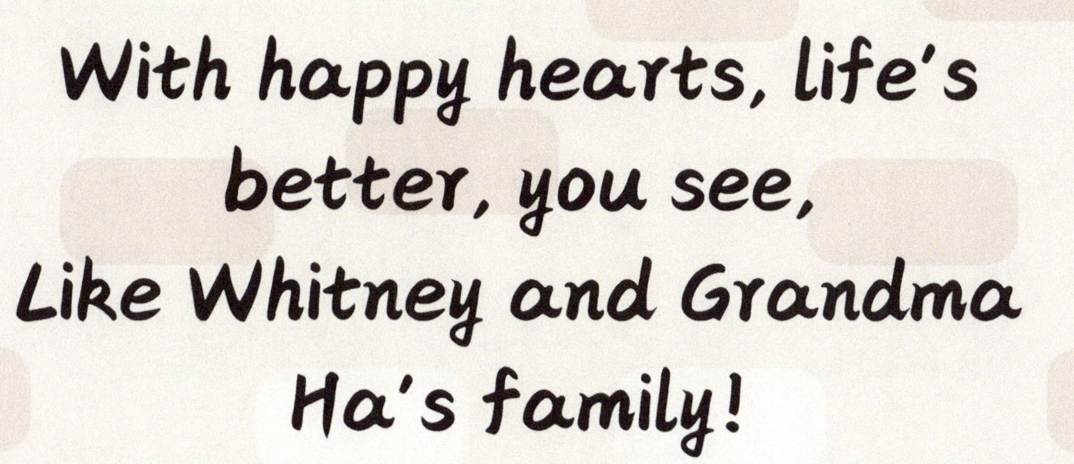

With happy hearts, life's
better, you see,
Like Whitney and Grandma
Ha's family!

And as the stars twinkle
in the night,
Whitney whispers,
"Ha, you're my light."

Bonus FREE
Activity Guide

Activity Guide

"Whitney Waits Tables (Sort Of!)"

Thank you for reading Whitney Waits Tables (Sort Of!) This guide is filled with fun activities to help kids connect with the story and learn about teamwork, gratitude, and the joy of helping out.

1. Draw Your Own Café Menu
Whitney made drawings for the café guests. Now it's your turn!
Materials Needed: Paper, crayons, or markers.
Instructions: Create a menu for your imaginary café. Include fun dishes like "Silly Spaghetti" or "Magical Milkshakes." Add colorful pictures of each dish.

2. Role-Play: Be a Waiter or Waitress
Just like Whitney, you can pretend to take orders!
Materials Needed: Notepad, pen, and a pretend dining area.
Instructions: Set up a small "restaurant" at home. Have friends or family pretend to be customers. Practice taking their orders and delivering "food" (use toy dishes or paper cutouts).

3. Gratitude Jar
Whitney learned the value of being grateful for her grandma. Let's make a gratitude jar!
Materials Needed: A jar, slips of paper, and a pen.
Instructions: Write down things you're thankful for on small pieces of paper. Add them to the jar. Read them together with your family at the end of the week.

4. Learn About Flint, Michigan
The story takes place in Flint. Let's explore its history!
Activity: Look up fun facts about Flint, Michigan. What is it known for? Draw or write about something you learned.

5. Design a Thank-You Card for a Grandparent
Grandma Ha loved spending time with Whitney. Make a card to show love to your grandparents!
Materials Needed: Paper, crayons, markers, or stickers.
Instructions: Write a heartfelt message and decorate your card. If you don't have grandparents nearby, make one for another special adult in your life.

6. Act It Out
Bring the story to life with a play!
Instructions: Assign roles—someone can be Whitney, Grandma Ha, and the café customers. Perform the story for family or friends.

7. Create Your Own Tip Jar
Whitney earned tips for her hard work. Make your own jar!
Materials Needed: A small jar, paper, and markers.
Instructions: Decorate the jar and use it to save money or collect "tips" for helping out at home.

8. Write a Thank-You Note to Someone Who Helps You
Whitney helped her grandma, and Grandma Ha praised her. Now it's your turn to show appreciation!
Instructions: Think of someone who helps you—a teacher, friend, or family member—and write them a thank-you note.

9. Recipe Time: Make a Dish with a Family Member
Cook together, just like Whitney and Grandma Ha!
Materials Needed: Simple ingredients for a family recipe.
Instructions: Pick a favorite recipe, and let an adult guide you in cooking or baking something yummy.

10. Discussion Questions
Talk about the story with family or friends.
What was your favorite part of the story?
How did Whitney show kindness and teamwork?
What's a time you helped someone, and how did it make you feel?
We'd love to see your activities!

Share your artwork, menus, and gratitude jars with us at
info@booksbyschaaf.com

Enjoy the magic of helping and learning, just like Whitney!

Join Our Book of the Month Club!

Looking for the perfect gift that keeps on giving? Join our Book of the Month Club! For just $25 a month, or $250 if you purchase a year upfront, you or your loved ones will receive a handpicked children's book every month, straight to your doorstep.

Here's how it works:
Choose from 15 different languages to receive bilingual books that make learning fun.
Enjoy monthly shipments of our exclusive books that inspire, teach, and entertain children of all ages.
Each month's book is carefully selected to provide a new adventure, valuable lesson, and a chance to explore cultures from around the world.
It's the perfect gift for birthdays, holidays, or just because! Whether you're nurturing a young reader or encouraging language learning, our Book of the Month Club is designed to bring joy to every bookshelf.

Exclusive Bonus: As part of your membership, you'll also receive a monthly podcast about our featured book delivered straight to your email! Listen in for behind-the-scenes insights, fun facts, and tips for making storytime even more magical.

Sign up today at www.Booksbyschaaf.com and start enjoying the gift of reading all year long!

Books By Schaaf

www.BookBySchaaf.com

Podcast series about our book on TikTok.

Activity Guide companion's for each storybook can be found on our website.

Find us at:

www.ingramcontent.com/pod-product-compliance
Lightning Source LLC
Chambersburg PA
CBHW041948140726
48006CB00002BA/555